Gillen

This booklet was written by Rory Gillen, founder of GillenMarkets, and is also available in eBook format (PDF, ePub or Kindle).

About Gillen

Gillen is a boutique investment advisor offering expert advice on the management of personal, pension and corporate monies. We place a strong emphasis on fully understanding our clients' needs, so that we can make informed decisions and plans, together.

We are investment advisors, not product sellers. Our investment solutions are structured to meet the specific needs of each individual client with minimum assets of €500k.

Our investment advisory fee structure aligns our interests with yours, ensuring that we sit on the same side of the table as our clients.

With our fee structure, there are:

- No upfront commissions or fees payable by clients.
- No dealing costs.
- No early redemption penalties.
- No VAT.

Just a transparent 1.0% annual advisory fee on the assets under advice.

We also offer a subscription-based investment newsletter for do-it-yourself investors and training courses both in-person and online for those wishing to learn more about the principles of sound investing.

We believe trust is earned. Our belief is that we work for clients, looking at each individual's needs and taking a commonsense, long-term approach.

We have built an outstanding team with the depth of knowledge and experience to meet all our clients' investment needs. We have an appetite for learning and sharing and we always partner with our clients as equals.

We'd like to hear from you!

Contact details

T: + 353 (0)1 287 1400
E: info@gillenmarkets.com
W: www.gillenmarkets.com

Follow us on Facebook, LinkedIn, Twitter and Gillenmarkets.com.

ILTB Ltd (trading as Gillen/GillenMarkets) is regulated by the Central Bank of Ireland.

Timing the Markets

Unemotional Approaches to Making Buy & Sell Decisions in Markets

A **GillenMarkets** Publication

Rory Gillen

Published by OAK TREE PRESS, Cork T12 XY2N
www.oaktreepress.com / www.SuccessStore.com

© 2023 ILTB Ltd t/a GillenMarkets

A catalogue record of this book is available from the British Library.

ISBN 978 1 78119 552 9 (Paperback)
ISBN 978 1 78119 553 6 (PDF)
ISBN 978 1 78119 554 3 (ePub)
ISBN 978 1 78119 569 7 (Kindle)

Disclaimer
Investing carries risk and none of the stocks or funds highlighted in this booklet constitute a recommendation by the author, GillenMarkets or the publisher and none of these parties can assume liability for any losses that may be sustained should a reader subsequently invest in them, and any such liability is hereby disclaimed. Readers should take professional advice before making any investment. None of the material in this publication constitutes investment advice or an offer to invest in any of the funds referred to. No one receiving this publication should treat it as a personal recommendation as it does not take into account the needs and objectives, personal circumstances, including investment experience, financial position, or attitude to risk of recipients.
Warning
Past performance is not a reliable guide to future performance.

CONTENTS

Gillen.

Other Publications from GillenMarkets

3 STEPS TO INVESTMENT SUCCESS (2012)
How to Obtain the Returns While Controlling the Risk

Rory Gillen

A PATH TO FINANCIAL FREEDOM (2nd edition / 2023)
A Guide to Sound Investing

Rory Gillen

BRICKS & MORTAR THROUGH STOCKS & SHARES (2023)
Property Investing in the Stock Markets

Darren Gillen

PRIVATE EQUITY: ACCESS FOR ALL (2023)
Investing in Private Equity through the Stock Markets

Jonathan Yates

INTELLIGENT GOLD INVESTING (2nd edition / 2023)
Including a Section on Bitcoin

Rory Gillen

UNDERSTANDING ALTERNATIVE ASSETS (2nd edition / 2023)
Gold, Forestry, Government & Corporate Bonds, Renewable Energy & Hedge Strategies

Rory Gillen

All available in print and ebook formats from
GillenMarkets.com, SuccessStore.com & Amazon

INTRODUCTION

In democratic and pro-business economies, the stock markets have historically delivered returns well in excess of bank deposits over five to 10-year timelines and have provided significantly greater liquidity (*i.e.* access to your assets at short notice) compared to investing in physical property like an apartment or a house.

But the markets can be volatile and not everyone wants that volatility or can take the time to ride out the inevitable market downturns.

Timing your entry into and exit from markets offers you a choice, but timing markets is not a silver bullet solution for investment success. Deciding to adopt a market timing strategy demands that you understand the approach and have the discipline to follow it through at times when it is not working to plan as well as through the good times.

If you follow the rules, however, you can most likely capture most of the returns normally offered by the stock markets while avoiding the downside risks associated with major and prolonged bear (declining) markets.

This booklet outlines three time-tested market timing indicators, as well as one that has an excellent, long-term history of identifying market bottoms.

The booklet also outlines the rules for how to follow or adopt each market timing indicator along with the track record of returns of the 'Buy & Sell' signals of each going back several decades.

Rules-based approaches to investing, such as the market timing indicators we put forward here, take much of the emotional ride out of making investment decisions. And you will most likely be a better investor for that.

Everyone is fearful at market bottoms, but a tried and tested market timing indicator can greatly assist you to see when the crowd has turned. Traditional and social media cannot help you – they are recording the economic news of the day and what investors are saying.

But what you want to know is: What are investors doing? If the selling is done and the average investor has turned into a buyer, you will see that in the price action of the market. Learn how to read the markets and you can stand aside from the crowd and make unemotional decisions at both market bottoms and market tops.

There are two possible ways to take advantage of the recurring wide fluctuations in stock prices, by way of pricing or by way of timing.

Benjamin Graham, *The Intelligent Investor* (1949, 1st Edition)

Ben Graham's quote above ranks as one of the very best I have read on investing. And here's my interpretation of it.

Recurring Wide Fluctuations in Stock Prices

Over the long-term, stock markets rise principally to reflect the growth in corporate earnings. For example, earnings for the 500 companies that make up the US S&P 500 Index have grown by 6.1% compound *per annum* from 1950 to 2022 inclusive, a 73-year period which we can accept as representative of the long-term.

The S&P 500 Price Index has gained 7.7% compound *per annum* over that same 73-year timeline. Not a perfect correlation with the underlying earnings growth but close enough to make the point. Share prices follow earnings over the medium- to long-term!

The nature of markets, however, is that they are volatile over short-term timelines (weekly, monthly, quarterly) and often rise well above the long-term earnings trend in good times, only to decline well below the long-term trend in earnings in more challenging times.

By Way of Pricing

GillenMarkets' approach to investing is to <u>own</u> assets for the medium- to long-term in order to benefit from the compounding of earnings, be that individual companies (stocks/shares/equities) or funds, and to try and avoid the three principal risks that can lead to permanent losses, which include:

- **The business risks:** The risks that a company's business model has deteriorated and that past levels of profitability are unlikely to be achieved again in the future.

- **The financial risks:** The risks of inappropriate financing and debt levels, which exposes the company to failure and investors to a potential total loss.

- **The valuation risks:** The risks of overpaying for the shares, which will lower the future returns that you can obtain from them.

In democratic economies with governments that are pro-business, stock markets and property values tend to make upwards progress over time, reflecting population growth and improvements in productivity driven by innovation and specialisation, which boosts corporate earnings and incomes.

To invest in assets with sound fundamentals, low risk and offering reasonable value is, as Graham outlines above, to invest 'by way of pricing'.

If the recurring wide fluctuations in stock prices offer up better value without any increase in the risk of a permanent loss of capital, then the investor should try and take advantage of such price fluctuations. In other words, it makes sense to buy when prices are lower.

By Way of Timing

But there is another way to take advantage of the recurring wide fluctuations in stock prices: 'by way of timing' or timing the markets. This booklet is aimed at providing readers with an understanding of how to time the markets and highlights some approaches to market timing that we have followed over the years and which you may find useful.

Timing the markets can form an investment strategy in its own right. If you choose, you can use the approaches outlined in this booklet to guide you as to when the probability is high that markets are in a defined uptrend or downtrend, thus assisting you to decide when you should be invested or when you should stay on the sidelines.

This, of course, may make better sense in a tax-efficient pension account where 'selling' does not crystallise a tax bill.

Using Technical Indicators, or Price Action, to Time the Markets

Technical analysis is the study of price movements or price action in markets in an attempt to determine the likely direction of them. Quite simply, if the direction is likely upwards, an investor who is timing the markets will want to be invested and if the likely direction is downwards, the investor will want to exit.

Price action, then, can be studied to determine what investors are actually doing, not what they are saying or what is being reported in traditional media or on social media. Occasionally, if correctly interpreted, the markets reveal where they are next most likely to go. As investors, we are all surely interested in understanding what the markets are saying, even if we don't make investment decisions based on price action but on company fundamentals.

As with investing based on fundamental analysis, technical analysis – or price action – is not a silver bullet solution for investing, and approaches to market timing do not offer up the Holy Grail of investing. Not all market timing signals lead to gains.

The idea that you can read the market signals – sell out before downturns and re-enter before upturns – is seductive. Many, who stand to gain from a higher-than-necessary level of investor activity, will try to convince you that it is easy to make money in markets that way; nothing could be further from the truth.

Both technical analysis and fundamental investing have advantages and disadvantages when used to make investment decisions and neither can be mastered without understanding, homework and discipline.

Only the Primary Trend is of Interest

As formulated by Charles Dow, founder of the *Wall Street Journal*, over 120 years ago, there are, simultaneously, three movements in progress in the stock market.

The main trend is referred to as the primary trend: the market is either in a medium-term upward or downward trend. In the midst of any primary trend there are the inevitable reactions against that primary trend, which are referred to as secondary movements. These are deceptive and represented by sharp declines in a bull (rising) market and sharp rallies in a bear (declining) market. Eventually, a secondary reaction becomes more than that and results in a change in trend from a primary bull market to a primary bear market (or *vice versa*).

Concurrently with the primary and secondary movements of the market are the daily movements, which represent the third type of trend or movement. Daily movements are largely irrelevant and, generally, no worthwhile inferences can be taken from them. The primary trend is key.

As this book is about investing and not speculating, we will be elaborating on technical indicators that provide clues regarding the primary trend of the market only. We will not be discussing or examining technical signals used to try and determine short-term market movements, as they are of use only to the speculator. Here, we are interested in catching the big moves – the switch from a primary bull market to a primary bear market (or *vice versa*) – and not the secondary or daily movements in between.

If you take the time to understand the language of the market, you will free yourself from having to react to every move the market makes, or from being dependent on outside commentators' interpretations of what is going on.

It is not the opinions of others that matter, no matter how intelligent they seem. The market itself is the opinion former: the market is made up of professional fund managers, professional traders, private investors, private speculators, market makers, stockbrokers, analysts and many other participants.

Quite simply, when buying outweighs selling, the market moves up, and when selling outweighs buying, the market moves down.

All the buyers are buying for reasons they feel are correct, based on information they have received or analysed. Similarly, sellers are selling for reasons they also believe to be correct. The point is that all the information that is out there is being interpreted by a myriad of different parties, and then expressed in the market. They are not expressing their opinions with words but with positive action (buying and selling). So, we can justifiably conclude that everyone's view is already – and always – in the market. That does not mean that the majority is always right, but it is the best guide we have regarding the likely market direction.

Looked at from this stance, if there is bad news on the economy heading our way, the majority view will sense that and express it in the market by increased selling – leading to a declining market. Likewise, when the economy is improving or has stopped deteriorating, then the majority will sense it and buying will outweigh selling – leading to a rising (or recovering) market.

Only the price action can tell when buying outweighs selling or when selling outweighs buying. This may sound like common-sense but, to see the market action in this way, one must remove one's own view and analyse the movements of the market in a cold, dispassionate way.

As everyone's view is in the market – and often these views are expressing things that are not yet obvious in the real economy – the market can be seen as a forward-looking indicator, pointing the way to improving or deteriorating economic and business conditions. For that reason, the stock market can be seen as a leading indicator of the likely business conditions ahead.

For example, after the sharp decline in global stock markets from mid-2007 to early-2009, a recovery in markets got underway in mid-March 2009. As I recall, at the time many commentators denounced the recovery as nothing more than a 'dead-cat bounce', but the market recovery continued. Enough investors had formed the view that central banks' and governments' policies would be sufficient to ensure economic recovery. When the majority positive view outnumbered the detractors, the market had to rise.

Back in mid-2009, investors got it right as the economy indeed started a recovery soon after, and the recovery justified their buying ahead of time. Hence, the stock markets foresaw the economic recovery that followed the Global Financial Crisis.

Many investors, particularly private investors, are bewildered when the market rises in the face of bad news in the media. Their mistake is not understanding that the bad news has probably already been priced in or discounted. If it has already been discounted and the news is even incrementally better, then that is reason enough for the market to rise.

The Technical Indicators

There are four technical indicators that we will outline in this booklet. For each, we will provide an understanding of how the indicator operates and highlight its track record over the long-term. The indicators are:

- The Capitulation Indicator.
- The Coppock Indicator.
- The 30- & 50-Week Moving Average Indicator.
- The Dow Theory for the 21st Century Indicator.

Both the 30- & 50-Week Moving Average and Dow Theory technical indicators provide 'Buy' and 'Sell' signals. In contrast, both the Capitulation and Coppock indicators provide 'Buy' signals only. So, if you are attracted to using the Capitulation Indicator and/or the Coppock Indicator for 'Buy' signals, you will need to use one of the other two indicators for 'Sell' signals.

In GillenMarkets, we don't use price action to make investment decisions. However, we recognise that the 'crowd' is far wiser in its understanding of where the markets are likely headed on a medium-term view than we are. So, we like to know what the markets are saying. There's an often-used stock market adage that states:

The stock market is the best guide to where the economy will be in six months' time, but you'll get nowhere looking at it the other way around.

In other words, you are not going to figure out where the stock market is headed by looking at the condition of the economy today. Many retail investors make that mistake and avoid stock markets when there is bad news on the economy.

Before we delve into the individual indicators, it might be worth providing some concrete examples of these indicators in action:

- In mid-March 2009, the global stock markets started to recover from a mauling that started in late 2007 and continued all through 2008 and into early March 2009, as the likely impact of the Global Financial Crisis on the banking system, corporate earnings and employment sank in with investors. Dow Theory had given a 'Sell' signal on the key

US equity markets in August 2007. The 30- & 50-Week Moving Average Indicator gave a 'Sell' signal on the key US equity markets in late January 2008. Where the US equity markets go, the rest normally follow. The dog tends to wag the tail!

- By starting a recovery in March 2009, the stock markets (investors) were saying that they were confident that central banks and governments were taking the appropriate action to ensure recovery. The markets were both correct in that view and early, as economic recovery duly started in late 2009. So, the stock markets often show the way. You just need to understand how to read the markets' signals.

  - At the end of February 2009, the Coppock Indicator gave a 'Buy' signal on the Chinese stock market.

  - On 23rd March 2009, Dow Theory[1] gave a 'Buy' signal on the key US equity markets.

  - At the end of April and May 2009, the Coppock Indicator gave 'Buy' signals on multiple stock markets around the world, thus confirming the earlier signal on the key US equity market given by Dow Theory.

  - Throughout the summer months of 2009, the slower moving 30- & 50-Week Moving Average Indicator gave 'Buy' signals on multiple equity markets.

- More recently, the Capitulation Indicator gave a 'Buy' signal on the key US equity markets on 24th December 2018, correctly signalling the end of the sharp decline that had occurred in the last quarter of 2018, as investors reacted negatively to the Federal Reserve's series of interest rate hikes at that time.

- In the midst of the Covid-19-induced stock market crash in late-February and March 2020, the Capitulation Indicator gave a rare 'Buy' signal on 9th March 2020. While the markets continued to sell-off for a further 10 days, a recovery started soon after, and the

---

[1] Jack Schannep's version of Dow Theory, known as Dow Theory for the 21st Century, gave a 'Buy' signal on 23rd March 2009.

markets never looked back despite Covid-19 shutting entire economies for many months.

- On 22nd February 2022, Dow Theory gave a 'Sell' signal on the key US equity markets signalling that investors saw trouble ahead. Russia invaded Ukraine on 26th February 2022 causing an energy crisis in Europe, amplifying the uptick in inflation that had ignited in many economies in early summer 2021, and leading to a rapid rise in interest rates in the developed world.

1: THE CAPITULATION INDICATOR

Understanding the Stock Market Cycles

*There are three principal phases of a bull market: the first is represented
by reviving confidence in the future of business; the second is the
response of stock prices to the known improvement in corporate
earnings, and the third is the period when speculation is rampant – a
period when stocks are advanced on hopes and expectations.
There are three principal phases of a bear market: the first represents
the abandonment of the hopes upon which stocks were purchased at
inflated prices; the second reflects selling due to decreased business and
earnings, and the third is caused by distress selling of sound securities,
regardless of their value, by those who must find a cash market for at
least a portion of their assets.*

Robert Rhea, *The Dow Theory* (1932).[2]

"Distressed selling of sound securities, regardless of their value, by those who must find cash for at least a portion of their assets" is capitulation. Robert Rhea, author of *The Dow Theory* (and following in the steps of Charles Dow and William Hamilton), didn't label such distressed selling as capitulation, but his quote above refers to that stage in markets where investors sell regardless of value.

Capitulation is a relatively rare event in markets and is generally a 'Buy' signal. Using Jack Schannep's Capitulation Indicator, capitulation in the US equity markets has occurred only 17 times since S&P 500 Index records began

---

[2]   Originally published by Barron's, 1932.

in 1953.The last capitulation event occurred on 9th March 2020 in the middle of the Covid-19 panic.

Capitulation is that point in markets where sellers overwhelm buyers as investors react to bad news, and share prices decline in rapid succession. History teaches us that when markets capitulate it is either the bottom of that particular correction, close to the bottom or the beginning of a bottoming process.

Capitulation in markets tends to happen at the end of bear markets where investors throw in the towel after a prolonged period of poor news flow. Capitulation occurred in late 1974 after a long bear market brought on by a surge in oil prices, inflation and a rapid rise in interest rates in the 1973-74 period. Capitulation similarly occurred in late 2002 and in late 2008 and early 2009 for the same reasons – consistent poor economic and business news flow.

Other capitulation events have occurred more suddenly when markets are hit by a shock – such as the Cuban Missile Crisis in 1962, the futures-driven Stock Market Crash of 1987, the terrorist attack on the Twin Towers in New York in September 2001 and the outbreak of Covid-19 in March 2020.

In this section of the booklet, we will examine two ways that capitulation can be measured in equity markets. No doubt there are other ways to measure capitulation, so that the approaches we highlight are unlikely to be exclusive.

The better indicator, in our view, is Jack Schannep's proprietary capitulation indicator. Jack Schannep is the former editor of 'thedowtheory.com' newsletter and also author of the book *Dow Theory for the 21st Century*. Schannep's indicator only records capitulation in the US equity markets.

However, as most of the global equity markets follow the US market's lead, at least in the short-term, a 'Buy' signal from Schannep's Capitulation Indicator on the US equity markets is normally a 'Buy' signal on most other global equity markets.

An alternative way to measure capitulation, and which works on any market, is to calculate the percentage decline in an index from its underlying 30-week moving average. Indeed, we successfully used this technique in early October 2016 to flag a potential bottom in the sterling exchange rate, and that subsequently proved to be the bottom of the sterling sell-off following the Brexit vote at end June 2016.

Schannep's Capitulation Indicator

Jack Schannep's capitulation indicator is a little more complex, but also more useful, we feel, for two reasons.

The first reason is that it uses a time-weighted moving average, so that it gives greater weight to more recent data compared to earlier data. From his book *Dow Theory for the 21st Century*[3] the actual definition of the Schannep Capitulation Indicator is:

> *A short-term oscillator is utilised which measures the percent of divergence between the three (US) major stock market indices (Dow Jones Industrial Average, S&P 500 and the New York Stock Exchange Composite) and their 10-week, time-weighted moving averages. Market bottoms are identified when the divergence between the three major (US) stock market indices is 10% below their respective 10-week, exponentially time-weighted moving averages.*

Most investors will not have the time or inclination to compute this in real-time themselves. So, if you want to follow Schannep's Capitulation Indicator, you will need to subscribe to his newsletter at **thedowtheory.com**. Alternatively, you can subscribe to **gillenmarkets.com** as we calculate capitulation levels ourselves and always send subscribers an email when a capitulation 'Buy' signal has been given.

The second reason is that the Schannep Capitulation Indicator has an excellent track record dating back to the start of the S&P 500 Index in 1953. Since 1953, using the Schannep Capitulation Indicator, US equity markets have capitulated on only 17 occasions and positive returns ensued following the vast majority of these 'Buy' signals.

The GillenMarkets website/newsletter service has been in operation since November 2009 and, over this timeline, we have witnessed three capitulation events in US equity markets – on 8th August 2011, 24th December 2018 and 9th March 2020.

---

[3]   *Dow Theory for the 21st Century*, Jack Schannep, John Wiley & Sons, Inc, Hoboken, New Jersey, USA, page 90.

Table 1: Capitulation in US Equities

Date	S&P 500 Level	Days from Actual Bottom	% from Actual Bottom	Returns – 6 Months Later	Returns - 1 Year Later
22-Jun-62	53	2	1%	19%	33%
25-May-70	70	1	1%	21%	42%
23-Aug-74	72	28	13%	16%	18%
30-Sep-74	64	3	2%	32%	32%
19-Oct-87	225	0	0%	15%	23%
03-Dec-87	225	1	1%	18%	21%
23-Aug-90	307	34	4%	19%	28%
31-Aug-98	957	0	0%	29%	38%
20-Sep-01	985	1	2%	17%	-7%
19-Jul-02	848	57	8%	6%	17%
09-Oct-02	777	0	0%	12%	34%
07-Oct-08	996	32	20%	-18%	12%
12-Nov-08	852	6	9%	6.6%	30%
23-Feb-09	743	10	8%	31%	47%
08-Aug-11	1,119	39	1%	14%	25%
24-Dec-18	2,417	0	0%	22%	26%
09-Mar-20	2,747	10	19%	24%	41%
Averages		**13**	**5%**	**17%**	**27%**

Source: **thedowtheory.com** / Bloomberg.

As *Table 1* highlights, following a Schannep capitulation 'Buy' signal, the average price return over the following six months from the S&P 500 Index has been 17% with only one period where a loss was recorded (-18% following the signal on 8th October 2008).

The average 1-year price return following a capitulation signal has been 27%, again with only one period where a loss was subsequently recorded (-7% following the signal on 20th September 2001[4]). In our view, these are

---

[4] A Dow Theory 'Sell' signal on 3rd June 2002 resulted in an investor exiting the S&P 500 Index for a 7% loss following the Capitulation Indicator's 'Buy' signal on 20th September 2001.

excellent odds and are the reason why capitulation in the key US equity markets is a 'Buy' signal, on average.

In deep bear markets, markets can capitulate more than once. So, it's safer to describe capitulation as signalling either the bottom (which it has done on four occasions since 1953), close to the bottom or the start of a bottoming process.

In late 2008, for example, during the Global Financial Crisis, US equity markets capitulated three times in succession – in October 2008, again in December 2008 and then for the last time in February 2009. So, on the first capitulation signal in October 2008, it was to prove subsequently that it was the start of a bottoming process on that occasion.

As **Table 1** also highlights, Jack Schannep's Capitulation Indicator gave its 'Buy' signals on average 13 days from the actual market bottom and on average within 5% of the actual bottom.

Knowing these odds might assist you to avoid selling when a capitulation signal has been given or, if you have the capacity to do so at such times, to make additional purchases.

The 30-Week Moving Average Capitulation Indicator

A moving average, like the 30- or 50-week moving average line, provides a smoothed picture of the underlying market trend. At times, the market moves ahead, sometimes far ahead, of the underlying trend. At other times, the market moves below, often far below, the underlying trend.

So, capitulation in a market can also be measured by calculating the percentage a particular market has declined relative to its 30-week moving average.

In effect, we are measuring the speed of decline and it is the *acceleration* in the price decline that highlights panic selling, which often occurs after a prolonged period of negative news flow. The selling continues until buyers emerge, thus finding the bottom of that particular sell-off. Because of the liquidity in markets, they tend to discount bad news quickly and for this reason markets often bottom months before the economy bottoms. The corollary is also true – stock markets peak well before the economy peaks.

Chart 1 highlights that, since 1950, a decline of 20% or more in the S&P 500 Index relative to its 30-week moving average represented an extreme market decline, as it has occurred on only seven occasions over that time frame.

Chart 1: S&P 500 Index: % Deviation from 30-Week Moving Average

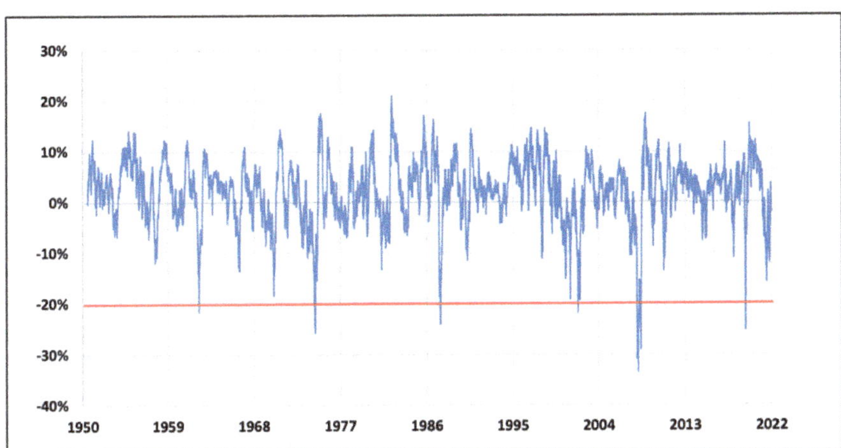

As ***Table 2*** highlights, price returns following a 20% decline in the S&P 500 Index relative to its 30-week moving average averaged 18.9% six months later and 25.2% 12 months later.

Table 2: S&P 500 Index: Capitulation – 20% Decline Below the 30-Week Moving Average

Date	Index Level	Returns	
		6 Months	12 Months
18-Jun-62	52.68	18.9%	33.4%
09-Sep-74	65.20	30.0%	27.8%
30-Nov-87	223.92	19.0%	21.4%
21-Sep-01	965.80	18.9%	-12.5%
19-Jul-02	847.76	6.4%	17.2%
10-Oct-08	899.00	-4.7%	19.1%
20-Mar-20	2,304.92	44.0%	69.8%
Average Return		**18.9%**	**25.2%**

However, there were far fewer 'Buy' signals over this 73-year timeline compared to Schannep's Capitulation Indicator. The subsequent returns following a 'Buy' signal using the 30-week moving average capitulation indicator were pretty much the same as for Schannep's Capitulation Indicator.

Hence, we conclude that it is the Schannep Capitulation Indicator that investors should adopt. Quite simply, it is the superior capitulation indicator. That said, many investors will find the 30-Week Moving Average Capitulation Indicator easier to compute and, therefore, easier to follow.

Of course, both capitulation indicators can complement each other as they provide reinforcing views and at alternative dates, albeit that the dates of the 'Buy' signals are close in all cases.

2: THE COPPOCK INDICATOR

Market folklore suggests that the Coppock Indicator was devised by Edwin Coppock, a US investment adviser, who had been approached by the Episcopalian church to advise it on when it was safe to re-enter markets. Coppock attacked the problem in a novel way and leaned into the field of human psychology for a possible answer.

He countered the church's question by asking the church how long it took, on average, for people to get over a bereavement. The church felt it took an average of 11 to 14 months. Coppock reasoned that it might take a similar period for investors to recover psychologically from a financial loss that bear markets bring on. He surmised that the negative impact of a bear market on an investor's appetite to take risk would be greatest at the time of a steep decline in markets, but progressively less negative as time passed.

The Coppock Indicator measures the pace of change between the most recent end-of-month index price and the index prices from 11 and 14 months ago. Said another way, the Coppock Indicator is an 11- to 14-month weighted-moving-average indicator, giving more weight to where the market is in the current month relative to 11 and 14 months ago and progressively less weight to where the market was 10 months ago relative to 11 to 14 months ago and so on.

It's easier to think in terms of an equal-weighted moving average, like the 30-week moving average, where you aggregate the index values for the last 30 weeks and divide by 30 to get a simple average. In the case of the Coppock Indicator, a higher (weighting) factor is applied to the more recent months' data, so that they are given more 'weight' in the decision.

The Coppock Indicator only gives 'Buy' signals as it is not designed to give 'Sell' signals. Nonetheless, as we will see, it has an excellent long-term track record of giving timely 'Buy' signals.

A Mechanical Approach Keeps Emotions Out of It

Similar to Schannep's Capitulation Indicator, the advantage of using a technical indicator like the Coppock Indicator is that an investor is not influenced by the unanimously bearish (or negative) sentiment that is always evident in and around market bottoms. Technical indicators cut through the 'noise' and let you see clearly what investors are actually doing, and not what they are saying and what is being reported in traditional and on social media.

Coppock 'Buy' signals are quite rare. For example, there have been only 19 'Buy' signals on the S&P 500 Index since 1950, a period spanning 73 years.

When Are Buy Signals Given?

The Coppock Indicator is a monthly indicator. A 'Buy' signal is given when the Coppock Indicator[5] drops below zero and then turns upwards from a negative position. As **Chart 2** shows, the last buy signal on the S&P 500 Index was given at the end of May 2016 when the indicator turned upwards from a very modestly negative reading.

As a consequence of the 2022 bear market in US equities, the Coppock Indicator on the S&P 500 Index is in negative territory at the time of this publication. A less negative reading will give a 'Buy' signal but that has not occurred at the time of writing.

As **Table 3** highlights, the Coppock Indicator has worked exceptionally well on the key US S&P 500 Index over many years. However, like many technical indicators, the Coppock Indicator does not work all the time.

---

[5]   **Appendix I** explains how to calculate the Coppock Indicator.

Chart 2: S&P 500 Index & Coppock Indicator (1950-2022)

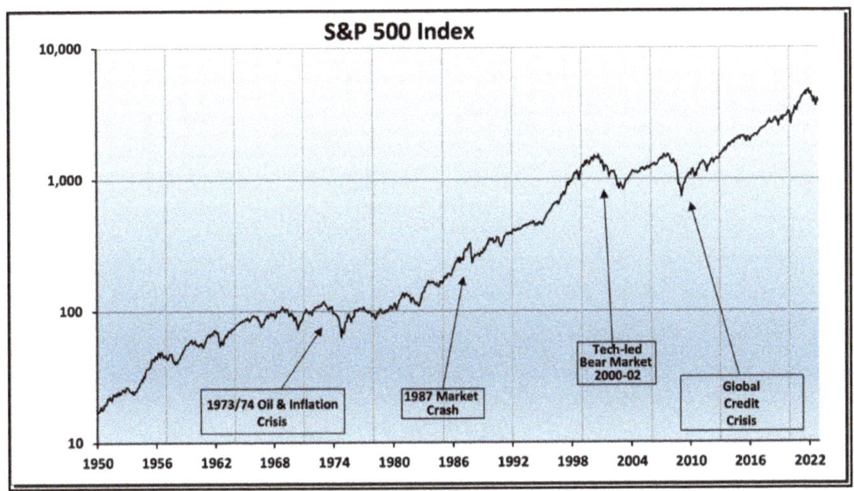

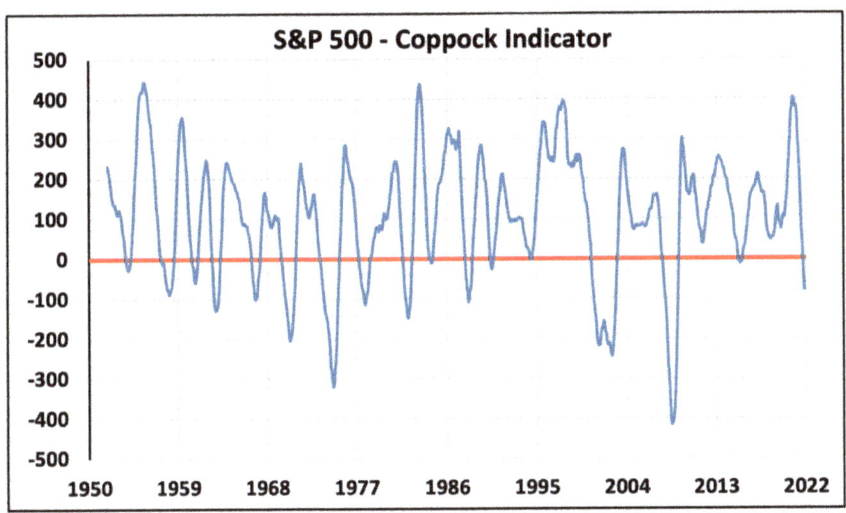

Source: GillenMarkets & Bloomberg.

Table 3: The Coppock Indicator – Signals on S&P 500 Index since 1950

Date	S&P 500 Level	Subsequent Returns		
		1 Year	3 Years	5 Years
29-Jan-54	26.08	40.5%	71.5%	112.5%
31-Jul-57	47.91	-1.5%	15.9%	21.5%
30-Apr-58	43.44	32.6%	50.3%	60.7%
30-Dec-60	58.11	23.1%	29.1%	59.1%
31-Jan-63	66.2	16.4%	40.3%	39.3%
31-Jan-67	86.61	6.5%	-1.0%	20.1%
31-Aug-70	81.0	22.4%	28.8%	8.4%
31-Jan-75	77.8	29.6%	15.6%	47.9%
30-Apr-78	98	4.1%	35.9%	66.0%
31-Aug-82	118	38.9%	59.5%	173.5%
31-Dec-84	167	26.3%	47.7%	111.3%
30-Sep-88	271	29.3%	43.4%	70.0%
28-Feb-91	370	11.3%	25.4%	73.9%
31-Jan-95	470	35.7%	112.9%	199.6%
31-Dec-01	1,148	-23.4%	4.7%	23.5%
30-Nov-02	935	14.5%	33.7%	58.5%
30-Apr-03	916	22.0%	43.1%	51.3%
31-May-09	919	18.5%	39.1%	109.4%
31-May-16	2,097	16.3%	31.8%	100.5%
Average Returns		**19.1%**	**38.3%**	**74.0%**

Table 3 provides an analysis of the price returns on the S&P 500 Index one, three and five years after a Coppock 'Buy' signal was given. Since 1950, there have been 19 Coppock 'Buy' signals given. In 17 out of those 19 occasions, the price returns from the market were positive one year later, and by an average of 19.1%.

After a three-year period, price returns were always positive, bar a modest negative return following the January 1967 'Buy' signal, with the average price return after three years clocking in at 38.3%. After a five-year period, the average price return has been 74.0% and there has not been a single 5-year period where returns were negative. Returns were higher if dividend income had been included.

By any measure, these are exceptional batting averages. The Coppock 'Buy' signal in December 2001 was a rare exception as it delivered a negative return of 23.4% one year later. Perhaps that can be explained by the fact that the S&P 500 Index still was substantially overvalued following the peaking of the US equity bull market in early 2000. Despite the sell-off in the US equity market following the terrorist attacks in September 2001 and the subsequent rebound in late 2001 that led to the Coppock 'Buy' signal on 31st December 2001, the US equity market was not cheap enough to support a real recovery in prices.

Of course, we are looking at these statistics in hindsight, and, as ***Chart 2*** highlights, in hindsight the US S&P 500 Index made consistent upwards progress, so that returns were always biased to the upside. Where a stock market is mired in deflation, as occurred in Japan between 1990 and 2012, the Coppock Indicator will not work as well, which was the case on the Japanese Stock Market over that period. On several occasions between 1990 and 2012, 'Buy' signals from the Coppock Indicator on the Japanese stock markets led to losses after 3- and 5-year periods.

To conclude, the Coppock Indicator can be applied to any market, and the probability of positive returns is high following a 'Buy' signal, assuming there is an upward bias in that market over time.

3: THE 30- & 50-WEEK MOVING AVERAGE INDICATOR

A Slower but Reliable Signal

Here, we examine the combined 30- & 50-week Moving Average Indicator as a market 'Buy' and 'Sell' signal. This particular technical indicator was discussed at length in Mark Shipman's 2008 book, *Big Money, Little Effort*.[6]

Similar to other indicators discussed in this booklet, the 30- & 50-Week Moving Average Indicator is mechanical in nature, with no subjectivity or input required by the user, apart from using a spreadsheet.

The 30- & 50-week moving averages are calculated by obtaining the average price of the market over the last 30 and 50 weeks. Like any moving average, the 30-week and 50-week moving averages help iron out the short-term volatility in the market and can assist investors to more easily identify the underlying trend.

The defining characteristic of this indicator is that a 'Buy' signal is generated when the 30-week moving average line moves up through the 50-week moving average line. Similarly, a 'Sell' signal is given when the 30-week moving average line crosses down through the 50-week moving average line. In essence, it is signalling that the near-term momentum in a market has either turned upwards or downwards – in other words, the indicator is signalling a turn in the primary trend.

It is a slower moving indicator compared to the Capitulation Indicator, the Coppock Indicator and the Dow Theory Indicator. As a result, it gives fewer signals and tends to get an investor out of the market later into a downturn and back into the market later in a recovery. Nonetheless, it is an easy-to-use

---

[6]   Shipman, M. (2008). *Big Money, Little Effort: Practical and Effective Strategies for Stock Market Investment*, London: Kogan Page.

indicator and provides 'Sell' signals, so that it can be used alongside both the Capitulation and Coppock indicators, both of which provide 'Buy' signals only.

Chart 3 highlights the 30- & 50-week moving averages on the S&P 500 Index from 2016 to 2022 inclusive with the 30-week and 50-week moving averages in red and green, respectively.

Chart 3: S&P 500 Index: 30- & 50-Week Moving Averages

As you can see in *Chart 3*, both the 30- and 50-week moving averages were rising by mid-2016. With both averages rising, the probability that the market was in a defined uptrend was high and that probability is captured, and a 'Buy' signal triggered, when the 30-week moving average rose above the 50-week moving average. Similarly, by mid-2022 both the 30- and 50-week moving averages were declining, so that the probability that the S&P 500 Index was in a defined downtrend had risen significantly. That probability was captured, and a 'Sell' signal triggered, when the 30-week moving average declined below the 50-week moving average.

A Good Track Record

Like any other technical indicator, of paramount importance is whether it has a good track record of calling market turns or not.

Table 4: 30- & 50-Week Moving Average Buy & Sell Signals – S&P 500 Index (1950 – 2022)

Buy Signal	S&P 500 Level	Sell Signal	S&P 500 Level	Gain / Loss (%)
11-Dec-1950	18.39	03/08/1953	24.78	34.7%
23-Feb-1954	26.15	28/01/1957	44.62	70.6%
03-Sep-1957	44.68	02/12/1957	41.31	-7.5%
14-Jul-1958	45.77	23/02/1960	56.16	22.7%
19-Dec-1960	57.44	18/06/1962	52.68	-8.3%
04-Mar-1963	65.33	11/07/1966	87.08	33.3%
17-Apr-1967	92.3	29/04/1968	98.66	6.9%
10-Jun-1968	101.13	30/06/1969	99.61	-1.5%
18-Jan-1971	94.88	29/11/1971	97.06	2.3%
13-Mar-1972	107.92	02/07/1973	101.28	-6.2%
12-May-1975	90.43	28/03/1977	99.21	9.7%
14-Aug-1978	104.73	02/04/1979	98.97	-5.5%
16-Jul-1979	101.82	10/08/1981	132.49	30.1%
01-Nov-1982	142.16	12/03/1984	159.27	12.0%
19-Nov-1984	166.92	04/01/1988	243.46	45.9%
22-Aug-1988	259.68	22/06/1990	355.43	36.9%
07-Sep-1990	323.40	12/10/1990	300.03	-7.2%
03-May-1991	380.81	15/07/1994	454.16	19.3%
06-Jan-1995	460.68	05/01/2001	1,298.35	181.8%
13-Jun-2003	988.61	29/10/2004	1,130.20	14.3%
17-Dec-2004	1,194.20	31/01/2008	1,395.42	16.8%
11-Sep-2009	1,043.00	05/05/2010	1,226.00	17.5%
24-Dec-2010	1,257.00	14/10/2011	1,225.00	-2.5%
06-Apr-2012	1,398.00	16/10/2015	2,033.11	45.4%
15-Jul-2016	2,161.74	15/03/2019	2,822.48	30.6%
12-Jul-2019	3,013.77	17/07/2020	3,224.74	7.0%
23-Oct-2020	3,465.39	03/06/2022	4,108.54	18.6%

Table 4 provides a list of every 'Buy' and 'Sell' signal using this indicator over the 73-year period from 1950 to 2022 inclusive. There were 27 'Buy & Sell' signals over this period with 20 of those signals providing a positive return by the time a 'Sell' signal was given (three out of four, or 75%), while seven of the calls resulted in a negative return by the time a 'Sell' signal was given (or one in four).

A 75% batting average is highly respectable. In addition, as **Table 5** highlights, an investor was invested only 72% of the time, so that interest could have been earned in bank deposits while on the sidelines.

Table 5: 30- & 50-Week Moving Average – S&P 500 Index (1950 - 2022)
Summary Statistics

Total Months Invested	622
Total Months	865
% of Time Invested	72%
No. of Wrong Calls	7
No. of Correct Calls	20
% of Correct	74%
Worst Single Loss	-8.3%
Largest Gain	181.8%
Worst Cumulative Loss (Dec-60 - Jun-62)	-8.3%
S&P 500 Index Return over same period	16.3%

Chart 4 records the total return an investor would have achieved (excluding costs and ignoring taxes) for both the Buy & Hold investor and the market timer using the 30 & 50-Week Moving Average Indicator to time your entry to and exit from the S&P 500 Index over the 1950 to 2022 period.

Over this 73-year period, the Buy & Hold investor generated modestly better returns of 11.2% compound *per annum* compared to 10.9% compound *per annum* by following the 30- & 50-Week Moving Average Indicator. Nonetheless, through the long bear markets of 1966 to 1982, 2000 to 2003 and 2007 to 2009, the indicator kept an investor largely out of these steep market declines.

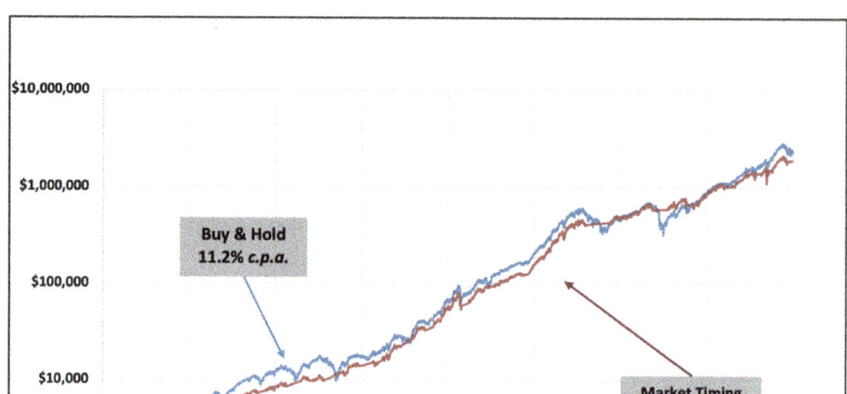

As ***Charts 5, 6, 7 & 8*** highlight, the 30- & 50-Week Moving Average Indicator on the S&P 500 Index saved an investor the significant drawdowns (declines) that were associated with the 1973-74, 2000-03, 2007-09 and the 2020-22 bear markets. Each chart covers a 10-year period. So, for an investor who cannot take the long-term view, the indicator has its attractions.

The indicator worked well for the 10-year period from 1969 to 1978. There were two bear markets in this difficult 10-year period for US equity markets – the first through 1969 and the second through 1973-74. Drawdowns for the 30- & 50-Week Moving Average Indicator were modest and yet the indicator captured a lot of the upside.

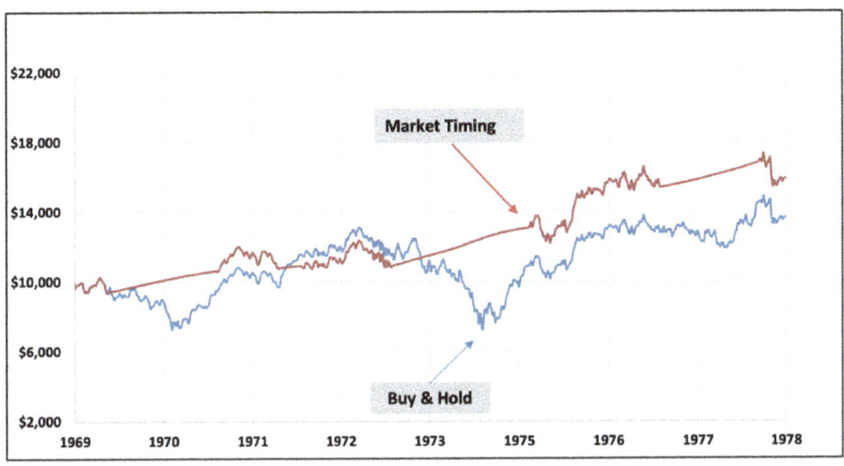

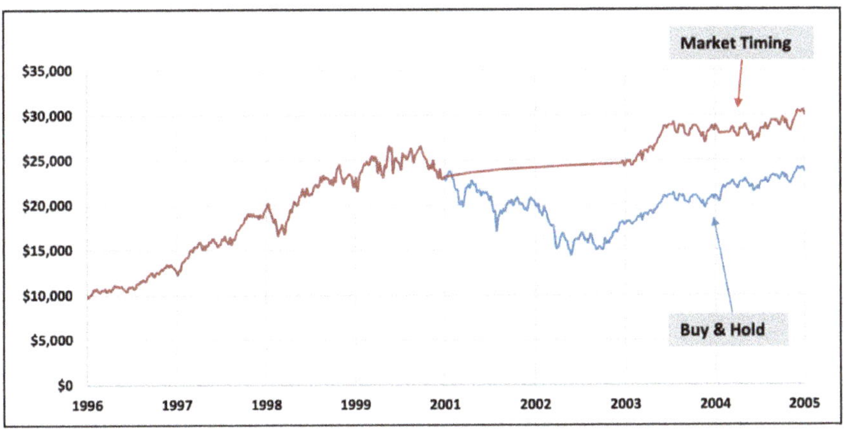

The indicator could do no wrong either in the 10-year period from 1996 to 2005. The reason for this is that the bear market of 2000 to early 2003 both started slowly and ended slowly, so that the slower moving 30- & 50-Week Moving Average Indicator gave timely signals. The result was that the indicator added significant value in this period.

Chart 7: S&P 500 Index (2003 – 2012) – Buy & Hold *vs* Market Timing
Value of $10,000 invested on 1st January 2003

In the 10-year period from 2003 to 2012, following the indicator resulted in reduced returns, but the drawdown (or initial loss) during the Global Financial Crisis was minimal. However, the US equity market recovery from the Global Financial Crisis was sharp, so that the 'Buy' signal coming from the 30- & 50-Week Moving Average Indicator was relatively late in September 2009 whereas the S&P 500 Index had bottomed in early March 2009 and started a V-shaped recovery at that time.

Similarly, in the current 10-year cycle (2016 to 2025) to date the indicator has led to reduced returns. The Covid-19 crash in global equity markets in March 2020 resulted in a 'Sell' signal in June 2020 on this indicator, yet the S&P 500 Index was clearly already back in an uptrend. More recently, the 30- & 50-Week Moving Average Indicator gave a 'Sell' signal in June 2022, so who knows what lies ahead for the remainder of this 10-year period.

Chart 8: S&P 500 Index (2016 – 2025) – Buy & Hold *vs* Market Timing
Value of $10,000 invested on 1st January 2016

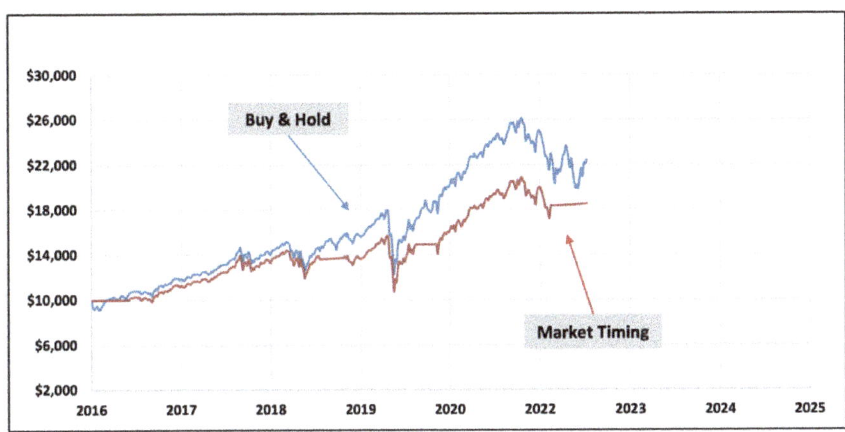

On a final note, we would highlight that this indicator has limited value in ranging markets (markets that are trading sideways with no defined uptrend or downtrend).

4: THE DOW THEORY FOR THE 21st CENTURY INDICATOR

A US Stock Market Barometer

During his years as the founder and first editor of the *Wall Street Journal*, Charles H. Dow formulated the theory that was later to be referred to as Dow Theory. William Hamilton, second editor of the *Wall Street Journal*, continued the use of this theory where Charles Dow left off, and subsequently wrote up the theory in *The Stock Market Barometer*, 1922.[7]

At its core there are three fundamental principles underlying Dow theory:

- **First Principle:** Everyone's view is in the market and their combined views are more powerful than any individual view. That being the case, the stock market itself tends to act as the leading indicator of what lies ahead for the economy and business.

- **Second Principle:** There are, simultaneously, three movements in progress in the stock market. The main trend is referred to as the primary trend: the market is either in a medium-term upward or downward trend. In the midst of any primary trend there are the inevitable reactions against that primary trend, and these are referred to as secondary movements. They are deceptive and represented by sharp declines in a bull market and sharp rallies in a bear market. Eventually, a secondary reaction becomes more than that and results in a change in trend from a primary bull market to a primary bear market (or *vice versa*). Dow Theory has a set of rules for judging when the tide has turned. Concurrent with the primary and secondary movements of the market are the daily movements that

---

represent the third type of trend or movement. Daily movements are largely irrelevant and, generally, no worthwhile inferences can be taken from them. The primary trend is key and secondary reactions must be watched closely for their potential to lead to a reversal of the primary trend.

- **Third Principle:** That the trend in the Dow Industrials Index must be confirmed by a similar trend in the Dow Transports Index. In other words, a possible change in the trend from a primary bull market to a primary bear market (or *vice versa*) must be confirmed by both indexes.

Dow Theory for the 21st Century

Jack Schannep, author of *Dow Theory for the 21st Century*, has brought the original Dow Theory up to date for developments in US equity markets over the past 100 years. Anyone interested in following Dow Theory for the 21st Century should read Jack Schannep's book and possibly subscribe to his newsletter at **www.thedowtheory.com**.

In January 1901, Charles Dow wrote the following to explain his theory:

> *A person watching the tide coming in and who wishes to know the exact spot which marks the high tide, sets a stick in the sand at the points reached by the incoming waves until the stick reaches a position where the waves no longer come up to it, and finally recede enough to show that the tide has turned. This method holds good in watching and determining the flood tide of the stock market.*

Where the US stock markets go, global stock markets tend to follow, in the short-term at least, so that the technical indicator, Dow Theory, has huge relevance beyond the US stock markets.

As with the previous technical indicators we have discussed, Dow Theory uses price action in an attempt to determine whether the US stock market's primary trend has changed from a bull to bear market or from a bear to bull market.

Lower Lows and Lower Highs Define a Bear Market

In price action terms, and in its very simplest form, the hallmark of a bear market is a series of lower lows and lower highs. Each low made in an ongoing bear market is succeeded by a new low later on (a lower low) and any secondary reaction in an ongoing bear market (for example, a rally against the primary downtrend) peaks out at a lower high than was previously made (a lower high).

Chart 9: S&P 500 Index: 2000 – 2003 Downtrend

As can be observed from **Chart 9,** each low in the 2000 to 2003 down-trending market (bear market) was followed by a lower low (black lines in **Chart 9**). And each time the S&P 500 Index rallied against that prevailing downtrend the high was lower than the previous high (a lower high – red lines in **Chart 9**).

Higher Highs and Higher Lows Define a Bull Market

Similarly, the hallmark of a bull market is a series of higher highs and higher lows. Each high made in an ongoing bull market is succeeded by a new high later on (a higher high) and any secondary reaction in an ongoing bull market (for example, a decline against the primary uptrend) bottoms out at a higher low than was previously made.

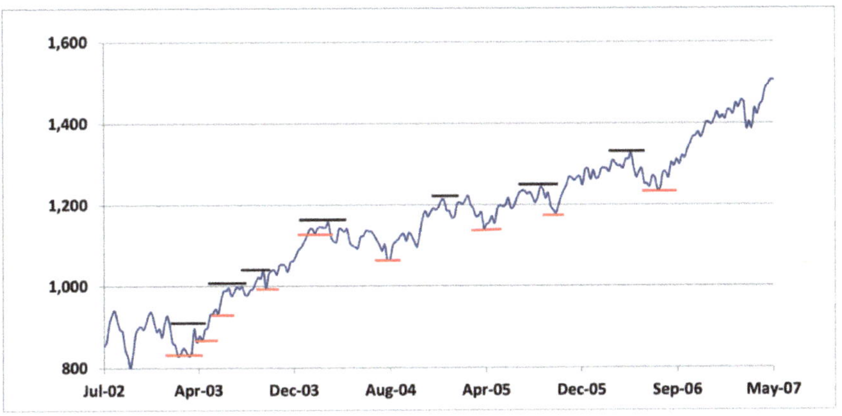

As can be observed from **Chart 10,** each high in the 2003 to 2007 upward-trending market (bull market) was followed by a higher high (black lines in **Chart 10**). And each time the S&P 500 Index declined against the prevailing uptrend, the low was higher than the previous low (a higher low – red lines in **Chart 10**). An exception to these rules occurred in August 2004, when lower lows were made.

Dow Theory for the 21st Century

Charles Dow used two indices – the Dow Jones Industrial Average Index (DJIA) and the Dow Jones Transports Index (DJTI) – insisting that a potential transition from bull to bear market (or *vice versa*) had to be confirmed by both indices before a signal that the market had turned was valid.

Jack Schannep's research, as outlined in *Dow Theory for the 21st Century*, highlights that a signal from the S&P 500 Index and at least one of the other two indices works best (for example, the S&P 500 Index along with confirmation from either the Dow Industrials or the Dow Transports Index). When Charles H. Dow formulated his theory, the S&P 500 Index did not exist (it was introduced in 1953).

The higher highs, higher lows principle (for bull markets) and the lower lows, lower highs principle (for bear markets) represent trending markets.

What Dow Theory attempts to do is determine when the primary trend has changed.

The exact rules for calling the turn in markets under Dow Theory for the 21st Century are numerous, and we don't intend to cover all the variations here, but we can summarise the major signals as follows:

Bull to Bear Market Sell Signals

- A secondary reaction in an ongoing bull market occurs when the S&P 500 Index plus one other index decline by more than 3% over a minimum of 10 calendar days on two of the three indices (S&P 500, Dow Industrials & Dow Transports) with at least eight trading days as the average for all three indices.

- The S&P 500 Index plus one other index must then rally at least 3%, but close below their previous highs.

- If the S&P 500 Index and at least one other index then decline again, and close below the previous lows, a 'Sell' signal is given.

- If during a decline, the markets don't rally the required 3% and the S&P 500 Index plus the Dow Industrials decline by 16% (Jack Schannep's definition of a bear market), a 'Sell' signal is also given.

Bear to Bull Market Buy Signals

- A secondary reaction in an ongoing bear market occurs when the S&P 500 Index plus one other index rise by more than 3% over a minimum of 10 calendar days on two of the three indices (S&P 500, Dow Industrials & Dow Transports) with at least eight trading days as the average for all three indices.

- The S&P 500 Index plus one other must then retreat by at least 3% and at least one index must close above its previous lows.

- If the S&P 500 Index plus one of the other two indices then rise again, and close above the previous highs, a 'Buy' signal is given.

- If during a rise, the markets don't decline the required 3% and the S&P 500 Index along with the Dow Industrials rise by 19% (Jack Schannep's definition of a bull market), a 'Buy' signal is given.

- In addition, when US stock markets capitulate – which often occurs late in bear markets – this is a partial 'Buy' signal under the rules of

Dow Theory for the 21st Century. Schannep's research has shown that a Dow Theory 'Buy' signal in the past has always followed capitulation, so he recommends that an investor commits 25% of his/her savings into markets on capitulation and before the likely follow-up and full 'Buy' signal from Dow Theory for the 21st Century.

Other events can influence 'Buy' and 'Sell' signals under the rules of Dow Theory for the 21st Century, and they are regularly discussed in Schannep's newsletter at **www.thedowtheory.com**.

The Track Record of Dow Theory for the 21st Century

Following a Dow Theory for the 21st Century 'Sell' signal, an investor's monies are assumed to be in cash earning the relevant interest rate pertaining at the time. We used US 3-month interest rates and assumed at least two weeks settlement before interest could be earned.

Table 6 outlines the returns from every 'Buy to Sell' round trip under the rules of Dow Theory for the 21st Century from the start of 1954 to the end of 2022, representing 69 years of data and compares the returns in each case to a 'Buy & Hold' strategy.

Table 6: Buy & Sell Signals (1954 – 2022) & Returns

	Buy Signal	S&P 500 Level	Sell Signal	S&P 500 Level	Gain/Loss
1	06-Jan-1954	25.14	05/02/1957	43.89	**75.1%**
2	21-Apr-1958	42.93	16/02/1960	54.73	**27.5%**
3	06-Mar-1961	64.05	12/04/1962	67.71	**5.9%**
4	22-Jun-1962	52.68	06/05/1966	87.84	**56.6%**
5	13-Dec-1966	82.73	02/11/1967	92.34	**11.6%**
6	24-Sep-1968	102.59	20/02/1969	99.97	**-2.6%**
7	16-Oct-1969	96.37	26/01/1970	88.17	**-8.5%**
8	25-May-1970	70.25	28/07/1971	97.07	**28.7%**
9	07-Sep-1971	101.15	26/02/1973	112.19	**10.9%**
10	23-Aug-1974	71.55	09/11/1976	99.32	**41.3%**
11	05-Jun-1978	99.95	17/10/1978	101.26	**1.3%**
12	04-Jan-1979	98.58	02/07/1981	128.64	**30.5%**

	Buy Signal	S&P 500 Level	Sell Signal	S&P 500 Level	Gain/Loss
13	20-Aug-1982	113.02	29/07/1983	162.56	**43.8%**
14	07-Oct-1983	170.80	03/02/1984	160.91	-5.8%
15	03-Aug-1984	162.35	12/10/1987	309.39	**86.9%**
16	19-Oct-1987	224.84	10/08/1988	261.90	**5.8%**
17	07-Oct-1988	278.07	13/10/1989	333.62	**20.0%**
18	02-Mar-1990	335.54	02/08/1990	351.48	**4.8%**
19	23-Aug-1990	307.06	04/08/1998	1,072.12	**248.0%**
20	31-Aug-1998	957.28	23/09/1999	1,280.41	**26.7%**
21	20-Sep-2001	984.54	03/06/2002	1,040.68	-2.4%
22	09-Oct-2002	776.76	24/01/2003	861.40	**5.0%**
23	22-Apr-2003	911.37	10/05/2004	1,087.12	**19.3%**
24	03-Nov-2004	1,143.20	14/04/2005	1,162.05	**1.6%**
25	18-Nov-2005	1,248.27	14/08/2007	1,426.54	**14.3%**
26	18-Apr-2008	1,390.33	02/07/2008	1,261.52	-9.3%
27	07-Oct-2008	996.23	17/02/2009	789.17	-15.4%
28	23-Feb-2009	743.33	04/06/2010	1,064.88	**35.2%**
29	15-Jun-2010	1,115.23	30/06/2010	1,030.71	-7.6%
30	26-Jul-2010	1,115.01	02/08/2011	1,254.05	**12.5%**
31	08-Aug-2011	1,204.49	03/10/2011	1,099.23	-5.9%
32	10-Oct-2011	1,194.89	21/08/2015	1,970.89	**64.9%**
33	07-Oct-2015	1,995.83	11/12/2015	2,012.37	**0.8%**
34	08-Jul-2016	2,129.90	23/11/2018	2,632.56	**23.6%**
35	24-Dec-2018	2,351.10	14/08/2019	2,840.60	**17.3%**
36	30-Aug-2019	2,926.46	25/02/2020	3,128.21	**6.9%**
37	09-Mar-2020	2,746.56	22/02/2022	4,304.76	**60.5%**
38	10-Aug-2022	4,210.24	15/09/2022	3,901.35	-7.3%
39	10-Nov-2022	3,956.37			

Table 7 outlines some summary statistics. As a timing indicator, Dow Theory for the 21st Century would have delivered a return of 13.6% compound *per annum* from 1954 to 2022 compared to 10.9% from a 'Buy & Hold strategy. These returns include dividend income reinvested in the Index.

Table 7: Dow Theory for 21ˢᵗ Century: Buy & Sell Signals – Summary Statistics

Strategy Return *c.p.a.*	13.6%
S&P 500 Returns *c.p.a.*	10.9%
Total Days	16,826
Number of Days Invested	12,659
% of Time Invested	75%
Number of Buy/Sell Trips	38
Number of Positive Outcomes	29
Number of Negative Outcomes	9
Maximum Loss	-15.4%
Maximum Sequential Loss	-24.7%

The following observations can be made:

- Adopting the Dow Theory for the 21ˢᵗ Century strategy led to 38 'Buy to Sell' roundtrips over this 69-year period. A positive return was generated in 29 out of the 38 trips, with a negative outcome recorded on nine of these occasions.

- This market timing strategy returned 13.6% compound *per annum versus* 10.9% compound *per annum* for the S&P 500 Index. These returns statistics include dividend income but ignore costs and taxes for the sake of simplicity.

- The S&P 500 Index's average annual dividend was in the order of 3.0% over this 69-year period.

- Had you adopted the Dow Theory for the 21ˢᵗ Century market timing approach, you would have been invested for 12,659 days out of the 16,826 days between the start of January 1954 and the end of December 2022. That's 75% of the time.

- Looking at the downside risks, the Dow Theory for the 21ˢᵗ Century strategy suffered a maximum decline in value of -15.4% in any single 'Buy & Sell' round trip and a maximum sequential loss of -24.7%. This compares to a maximum loss of -56.6% from peak-to-trough during the Global Financial Crisis-led bear market covering the period July 2007 to March 2009.

As *Table 8* highlights, adopting the Dow Theory for the 21st Century strategy outperformed a 'Buy & Hold' strategy in most decades with the exception of the 2010s.

Table 8: Returns per Decade (compound *p.a.*)

	Dow Theory Strategy	Buy & Hold Strategy	Out/Under Performance
1954-1959	20.1%	20.4%	-0.3%
1960s	8.6%	7.8%	0.8%
1970s	12.2%	5.9%	6.3%
1980s	20.5%	17.5%	3.0%
1990s	19.4%	18.2%	1.2%
2000s	6.5%	-0.9%	7.5%
2010s	11.6%	13.5%	-2.0%
2020s	13.4%	7.6%	5.8%
1954-2022	**13.7%**	**10.9%**	**2.8%**

Table 9: Bear Market Returns

Downturns	Peak-to-Trough Dates	Buy & Hold Strategy	Dow Theory (21C)	Out/Under Perfor mance
1973-74 Bear Market	11 Jan 1973 to 3 Oct 1974	-44.8%	-2.4%	42.4%
1987 Stock Market Crash	21 Aug 1987 to 4 Dec 1987	-32.6%	-7.4%	25.2%
2000-03 Bear Market	7 Apr 2000 to 9 Oct 2002	-47.0%	2.8%	49.8%
2007-09 Global Financial Crisis	5 Oct 2007 to 9 Mar 2009	-55.0%	-22.5%	32.5%
2020 Covid-19 Market Crash	12 Feb 2020 to 23 Mar 2020	-33.6%	-11.6%	22.0%

Table 9 is especially revealing as it highlights that the Dow Theory for the 21st Century strategy gained most of its outperformance in the three big bear

markets of the past 69 years, plus during the October 1987 stock market crash and the more recent Covid-19 panic sell-off in early 2020.

The peak-to-trough declines in the S&P 500 Index were:

- -44.8% in the 1973-74 bear market.

- -32.6% during the October 1987 stock market crash.

- -47.0% during the 2000-02 bear market.

- -55.0% during the 2007-09 Global Financial Crisis.

- -33.6% during the Covid-19 sell-off in Feb/March 2020.

The Dow Theory for the 21ˢᵗ Century strategy substantially outperformed during all five bear markets.

Annual Out/Under Performance

Chart 11 highlights the annual out/under performance of Dow Theory for the 21ˢᵗ Century compared to a 'Buy & Hold' strategy on the S&P 500 Index.

The strategy underperformed a 'Buy & Hold' strategy in 23 out of the 69 years (1/3ʳᵈ of the time), performed in line with the S&P 500 Index in 23 out of the 69 years and outperformed in 23 out of the 69 years.

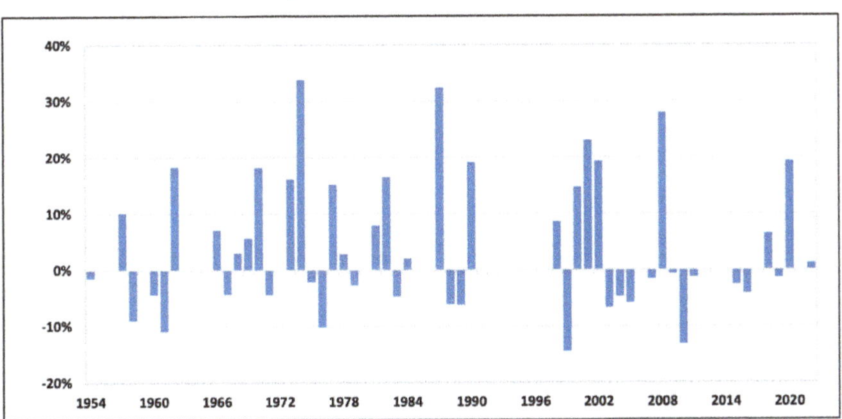

Chart 11: Dow Theory *vs* S&P 500: Annual Out/Under Performance

The Value of $10,000 Invested on 1st January 1954

Chart 12 highlights the progress of $10,000 invested on 1 January 1954 in both the Dow Theory for the 21st Century Strategy and the 'Buy & Hold' strategy.

Chart 12: S&P 500 *vs* Dow Theory for 21st Century (semi-log chart)

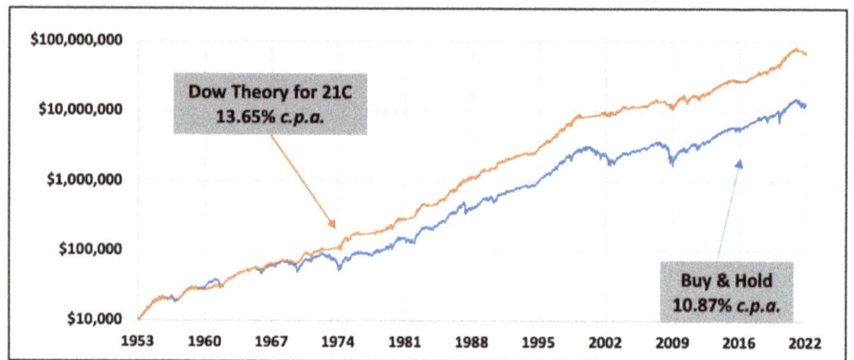

A $10,000 investment in the Dow Theory for the 21st Century strategy on 1st January 1954 would have grown to $68.1 million by end December 2022, representing a 13.65% compound *per annum* return over this 69-year period (including dividend income received but ignoring costs and taxes).

A similar $10,000 in the S&P 500 Index 'Buy & Hold' strategy would be worth $12.4 million today, representing a 10.87% compound *per annum* return over this same 69-year period (also including dividend income received but ignoring costs and taxes).

Compared to Hedge & Absolute Return Funds

Despite the glamour around hedge and absolute return funds, the reality is that, in aggregate, they have failed to live up to the hype.

As highlighted in ***Chart 13***, using HFRX indices[8] returns data from 1998 to 2022 inclusive, the average hedge fund only marginally beat bank deposit

---

[8]   HFRX indices are published by Hedge Fund research and available at
       https://www.hfr.com/family-indices/hfrx#.

returns, delivering a 3.9% compound *per annum* return over this 25-year timeline.

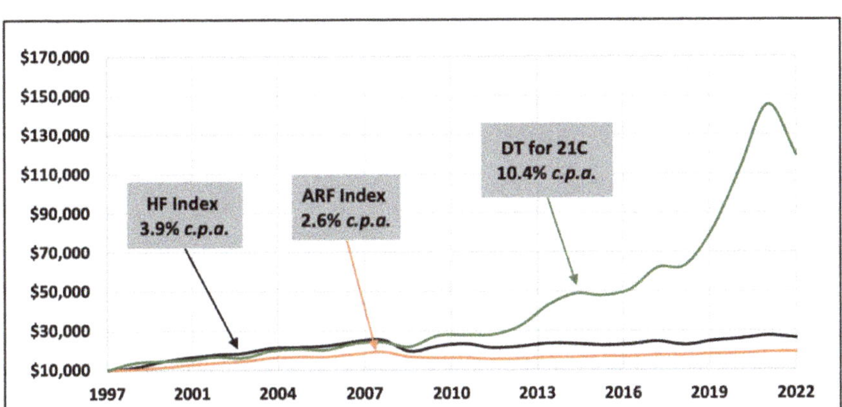

Chart 13: Dow Theory *vs* Hedge & Absolute Return Strategies
Value of $10,000 invested on 1st January 1998

In contrast, over the same timeline the Dow Theory strategy delivered a 10.4% compound *per annum* return.

Absolute return funds fared even less well, with the average absolute return fund, as tracked by the HFRX Indices, delivering a 2.6% compound *per annum* return from 1998 to 2022 inclusive.

The performance of absolute return funds in aggregate is particularly relevant. After all, at its core, Dow Theory for the 21st Century is about limiting the downside risk in markets while participating in the upside as much as possible. In that regard, the evidence over a long period of time is that Dow Theory achieves its aims, whereas the universe of absolute return funds has singularly failed to do so.

If we were to pass judgment on why the hedge and absolute return funds industry fails to deliver on its goals, we might conclude that they are failed attempts to actively manage monies across the various asset classes.

Compared to Multi-Asset Funds

In contrast, even the simple passively managed, multi-asset fund – equally weighted across the five major asset classes of global equities, fixed income government bonds, inflation-linked government bonds, bank deposits and gold – generated better returns than the hedge and absolute returns fund universe.

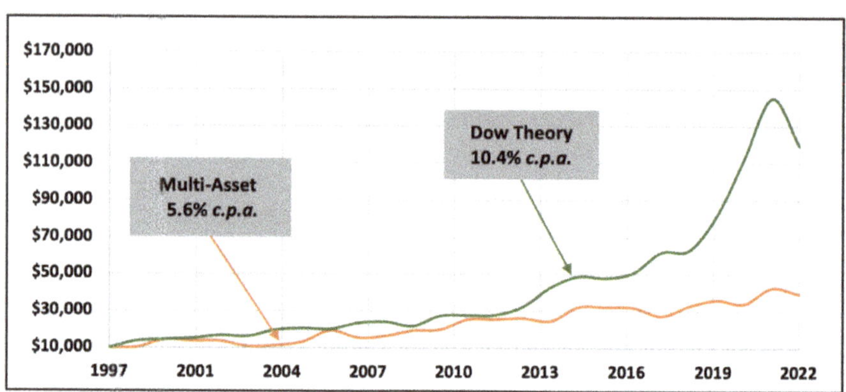

Chart 14: Dow Theory *vs* Multi-Asset Strategy
Value of $10,000 invested on 1st January 1998

As **Chart 14** highlights, an equally weighted multi-asset fund delivered a 5.6% compound *per annum* return over the same 1998 to 2022 timeline compared to 3.9% for the hedge funds universe and 2.6% for the absolute return funds universe.

And it's worth emphasising that a traditional multi-asset fund automatically covers the major economic risks for an investor – the risks of deflation (by owning fixed income government bonds), the risks of inflation (by owning inflation-linked government bonds), the risks of recessions (by owning bank deposits – interest rates normally rise ahead of a recession) and the risks associated with political instability and even wars (by owning gold).

However, even the multi-asset approach was no match for the Dow Theory for the 21st Century market timing indicator, which delivered a 10.4% compound *per annum* return over this same 25-year timeline.

Summary Comments

With a maximum single loss of 15.4% and a maximum sequential loss of 24.7% on any full 'Buy to Sell' round trip (which occurred during the Global Financial Crisis), the technical indicator Dow Theory for the 21ˢᵗ Century has proven itself over the long-term to limit the downside volatility in US equity markets more times than not. In particular, it did an excellent job of avoiding the bulk of the large declines suffered in the three worst bear markets of the last 69 years – the 1973 to 1974, 2000 to 2003 and 2007 to 2009 bear markets. The indicator even assisted investors to avoid the 1987 stock market crash and the Covid-19 related severe market sell-off.

Indeed, the major outperformance by the Dow Theory for the 21ˢᵗ Century strategy over a 'Buy & Hold' strategy largely comes down to its ability to avoid the sharp declines in these deep bear markets. Lastly, returns have benefitted from an understanding of 'Capitulation' in markets and the inclusion of capitulation as an initial 'Buy' signal under the rules of Dow Theory for the 21ˢᵗ Century. From a tax perspective, the strategy is clearly better utilised in tax-efficient accounts.

Appendix I: COPPOCK INDICATOR CALCULATIONS

For the index of your choice, the following guidelines should allow you to create your own Coppock Indicator. The next page has the actual calculations for the Euro Stoxx 50 Index leading up to the 'Buy' signal at the end of January 2023.

1. In Columns 1 & 2, note the end of month date and the value of the index for the previous 14 months.
2. In Column 3, note the index value for 14 months ago. In Column 4, express that difference as a percentage.
3. In Column 5, note the index value for 11 months ago. In Column 6, express that difference as a percentage.
4. In Column 7, add the 14- and 11-month percentage differences.
5. In Column 8, multiply Column 7 by 10.
6. In Column 9, drop down a month and multiply Column 7 by 9.
7. In Column 10, drop down a month and multiply Column 7 by 8.
8. And so on – in each successive Column, drop down a month and multiply by one less until you come to Column 18.
9. In Column 18, sum Columns 8 to 17.
10. In Column 19, divide Column 18 by 10.
11. After point 10, you have a weighted average of the end of month data stretching back 24 months.
12. Only readings that have a value for each of the Columns 8 to 17 are included in the series.
13. Now plot the series on a chart (optional).
14. The indicator provides a buy signal when it dips below zero and then gives a less negative reading.

Euro Stoxx 50 Index - Coppock Spreadsheet Example

1	2	3	4	5	6	7	8	9	10	11	12	13	14	15	16	17	18	19
		14m	%Δ	11m	%Δ	Add 2+4	Col7 X10	Col7 -1mx9	Col7 -2mx9	Col7 -3mx9	Col7 -4mx9	Col7 -5mx9	Col7 -6m x9	Col7 -7m x9	Col7 -8m x9	Col7 -9m x9	Sum Col8 -Col10	Divide Col18 by 10
31/07/ 2019	3,466.9																	
31/08/ 2019	3,426.8																	
30/09/ 2019	3,569.5																	
31/10/ 2019	3,604.4																	
30/11/ 2019	3,703.6																	
31/12/ 2019	3,745.2																	
31/01/ 2020	3,640.9																	
29/02/ 2020	3,329.5																	
31/03/ 2020	2,786.9																	
30/04/ 2020	2,927.9																	
31/05/ 2020	3,050.2																	
30/06/ 2020	3,234.0																	
31/07/ 2020	3,174.3																	
31/08/ 2020	3,272.5																	
30/09/ 2020	3,193.6	3,466.9	-7.9	3604.4	-11.4	-19.3	-192.8											
31/10/ 2020	2,958.0	3,426.8	-13.7	3703.6	-20.1	-33.8	-338.1	-173.5										
30/11/ 2020	3,492.5	3,569.5	-2.2	3745.2	-6.7	-8.9	-89.0	-304.3	-154.2									
31/12/ 2020	3,553.0	3,604.4	-1.4	3640.9	-2.4	-3.8	-38.4	-80.1	-270.5	-135.0								
31/01/ 2021	3,481.4	3,703.6	-6.0	3329.5	4.6	-1.4	-14.4	-34.6	-71.2	-236.7	-115.7							
28/02/ 2021	3,636.4	3,745.2	-2.9	2786.9	30.5	27.6	275.8	-12.9	-30.7	-62.3	-202.9	-96.4						
31/03/ 2021	3,919.2	3,640.9	7.6	2927.9	33.9	41.5	415.0	248.2	-11.5	-26.9	-53.4	-169.1	-77.1					
30/04/ 2021	3,974.7	3,329.5	19.4	3050.2	30.3	49.7	496.9	373.5	220.6	-10.1	-23.0	-44.5	-135.2	-57.8				
31/05/ 2021	4,039.5	2,786.9	44.9	3234.0	24.9	69.9	698.5	447.2	332.0	193.1	-8.6	-19.2	-35.6	-101.4	-38.6			
30/06/ 2021	4,064.3	2,927.9	38.8	3174.3	28.0	66.9	668.5	628.7	397.5	290.5	165.5	-7.2	-15.4	-26.7	-67.6	-19.3	2014.5	201.5
31/07/ 2021	4,089.3	3,050.2	34.1	3272.5	25.0	59.0	590.3	601.7	558.8	347.8	249.0	137.9	-5.7	-11.5	-17.8	-33.8	2416.6	241.7
31/08/ 2021	4,196.4	3,234.0	29.8	3193.6	31.4	61.2	611.6	531.2	534.8	489.0	298.1	207.5	110.3	-4.3	-7.7	-8.9	2761.7	276.2
30/09/ 2021	4,048.1	3,174.3	27.5	2958.0	36.9	64.4	643.8	550.4	472.2	468.0	419.1	248.5	166.0	82.7	-2.9	-3.8	3044.0	304.4
31/10/ 2021	4,250.6	3,272.5	29.9	3492.5	21.7	51.6	515.9	579.4	489.3	413.2	401.1	349.3	198.8	124.5	55.2	-1.4	3125.1	312.5
30/11/ 2021	4,063.1	3,193.6	27.2	3553.0	14.4	41.6	415.8	464.3	515.0	428.1	354.2	334.3	279.4	149.1	83.0	27.6	3050.7	305.1

1	2	3	4	5	6	7	8	9	10	11	12	13	14	15	16	17	18	19
		14m	%Δ	11m	%Δ	Add 2+4	Col7 X10	Col7 -1mx9	Col7 -2mx9	Col7 -3mx9	Col7 -4mx9	Col7 -5mx9	Col7 -6m x9	Col7 -7m x9	Col7 -8m x9	Col7 -9m x9	Sum Col8 -Col10	Divide Col18 by 10
31/12/ 2021	4,298.4	2,958.0	45.3	3481.4	23.5	68.8	687.8	374.2	412.7	450.7	367.0	295.1	267.4	209.6	99.4	41.5	3205.4	320.5
31/01/ 2022	4,174.6	3,492.5	19.5	3636.4	14.8	34.3	343.3	619.0	332.6	361.1	386.3	305.8	236.1	200.6	139.7	49.7	2974.2	297.4
28/02/ 2022	3,924.2	3,553.0	10.4	3919.2	0.1	10.6	105.8	309.0	550.3	291.1	309.5	321.9	244.6	177.1	133.7	69.9	2512.8	251.3
31/03/ 2022	3,902.5	3,481.4	12.1	3974.7	-1.8	10.3	102.8	95.2	274.6	481.5	249.5	258.0	257.5	183.5	118.1	66.9	2087.4	208.7
30/04/ 2022	3,802.9	3,636.4	4.6	4039.5	-5.9	-1.3	-12.8	92.5	84.6	240.3	412.7	207.9	206.4	193.1	122.3	59.0	1606.1	160.6
31/05/ 2022	3,789.2	3,919.2	-3.3	4064.3	-6.8	-10.1	-100.9	-11.5	82.2	74.0	206.0	343.9	166.3	154.8	128.8	61.2	1104.8	110.5
30/06/ 2022	3,454.9	3,974.7	-13.1	4089.3	-15.5	-28.6	-285.9	-90.8	-10.2	72.0	63.5	171.6	275.1	124.7	103.2	64.4	487.5	48.8
31/07/ 2022	3,708.1	4,039.5	-8.2	4196.4	-11.6	-19.8	-198.4	-257.3	-80.7	-9.0	61.7	52.9	137.3	206.3	83.2	51.6	47.6	4.8
31/08/ 2022	3,517.3	4,064.3	-13.5	4048.1	-13.1	-26.6	-265.7	-178.6	-228.8	-70.6	-7.7	51.4	42.3	103.0	137.6	41.6	-375.5	-37.5
30/09/ 2022	3,318.2	4,089.3	-18.9	4250.6	-21.9	-40.8	-407.9	-239.2	-158.7	-200.2	-60.5	-6.4	41.1	31.7	68.7	68.8	-862.6	-86.3
31/10/ 2022	3,617.5	4,196.4	-13.8	4063.1	-11.0	-24.8	-247.6	-367.1	-212.6	-138.9	-171.6	-50.4	-5.1	30.8	21.2	34.3	-1107.0	-110.7
30/11/ 2022	3,964.7	4,048.1	-2.1	4298.4	-7.8	-9.8	-98.2	-222.8	-326.3	-186.0	-119.0	-143.0	-40.3	-3.8	20.6	10.6	-1108.5	-110.8
31/12/ 2022	3,793.6	4,250.6	-10.8	4174.6	-9.1	-19.9	-198.8	-88.4	-198.1	-285.5	-159.4	-99.2	-114.4	-30.3	-2.6	10.3	-1166.3	-116.6
31/01/ 2023	4,163.5	4,063.1	2.5	3,924.2	6.1	8.6	85.7	-178.9	-78.9	-173.3	-244.7	-132.9	-79.4	-85.8	-20.2	-1.3	-909.3	-90.9

S&P 500 Index – SPREADSHEET Example

Date	S&P 500 Price Index	30-Week Moving Average	50-Week Moving Average
05-Nov-21	4,697.53		
12-Nov-21	4,682.85		
19-Nov-21	4,697.96		
26-Nov-21	4,594.62		
03-Dec-21	4,538.43		
10-Dec-21	4,712.02		
17-Dec-21	4,620.64		
24-Dec-21	4,725.79		
31-Dec-21	4,766.18		
07-Jan-22	4,677.03		
14-Jan-22	4,662.85		
21-Jan-22	4,397.94		
28-Jan-22	4,431.85		
04-Feb-22	4,500.53		
11-Feb-22	4,418.64		
18-Feb-22	4,348.87		
25-Feb-22	4,384.65		
04-Mar-22	4,328.87		
11-Mar-22	4,204.31		
18-Mar-22	4,463.12		
25-Mar-22	4,543.06		
01-Apr-22	4,545.86		

Date	S&P 500 Price Index	30-Week Moving Average	50-Week Moving Average
08-Apr-22	4,488.28		
15-Apr-22	4,393.00		
22-Apr-22	4,271.78		
29-Apr-22	4,131.93		
06-May-22	4,123.34		
13-May-22	4,023.89		
20-May-22	3,901.36		
27-May-22	4,158.00	4,447.84	
03-Jun-22	4,108.54	4,428.21	
10-Jun-22	3,901.00	4,402.14	
17-Jun-22	3,674.84	4,368.04	
24-Jun-22	3,911.74	4,345.28	
01-Jul-22	3,825.33	4,321.51	
08-Jul-22	3,899.38	4,294.42	
15-Jul-22	3,863.16	4,269.17	
22-Jul-22	3,961.63	4,243.70	
29-Jul-22	4,130.29	4,222.50	
12-Aug-22	4,280.15	4,192.02	
19-Aug-22	4,228.48	4,186.37	
26-Aug-22	4,057.66	4,173.90	
02-Sep-22	3,924.26	4,154.69	
09-Sep-22	4,067.36	4,142.98	
16-Sep-22	3,873.33	4,127.13	
23-Sep-22	3,693.23	4,104.08	
30-Sep-22	3,585.62	4,079.30	
07-Oct-22	3,639.66	4,060.48	
14-Oct-22	3,583.07	4,031.15	
21-Oct-22	3,752.75	4,004.80	4,216.89
28-Oct-22	3,901.06	3,983.31	4,201.25
04-Nov-22	3,770.55	3,959.39	4,182.70
11-Nov-22	3,992.93	3,946.05	4,170.67
18-Nov-22	3,965.35	3,935.84	4,159.21

Date	S&P 500 Price Index	30-Week Moving Average	50-Week Moving Average
25-Nov-22	4,026.12	3,932.31	4,145.49
02-Dec-22	4,071.70	3,930.59	4,134.51
09-Dec-22	3,976.68	3,929.01	4,119.53
16-Dec-22	3,852.36	3,927.38	4,101.25
23-Dec-22	3,836.00	3,916.65	4,084.43
30-Dec-22	3,839.50	3,907.68	4,067.96

Timing the Markets

The surest way to obtain the superior returns that stock markets have delivered in the past is to be an owner of "assets", either through a diversified selection of individual companies or through funds. However, not everyone has the patience or, indeed, the time to be a 'Buy & Hold' investor.

Technical analysis is the study of price movements or price action in markets in an attempt to determine their likely future direction. Quite simply, if the direction is likely upwards, an investor who is timing the markets will want to be invested and if the likely direction is downwards, the investor will want to exit.

Written by Rory Gillen, founder of GillenMarkets and author of *3 Steps to Investment Success*, published in 2012, this booklet aims to provide readers with an understanding of how to time the markets and highlights a couple of successful technical indicators to market timing that we have followed over the years.

Gillen.

E: info@gillenmarkets.com
T: +353 1 2871400
W: www.gillenmarkets.com